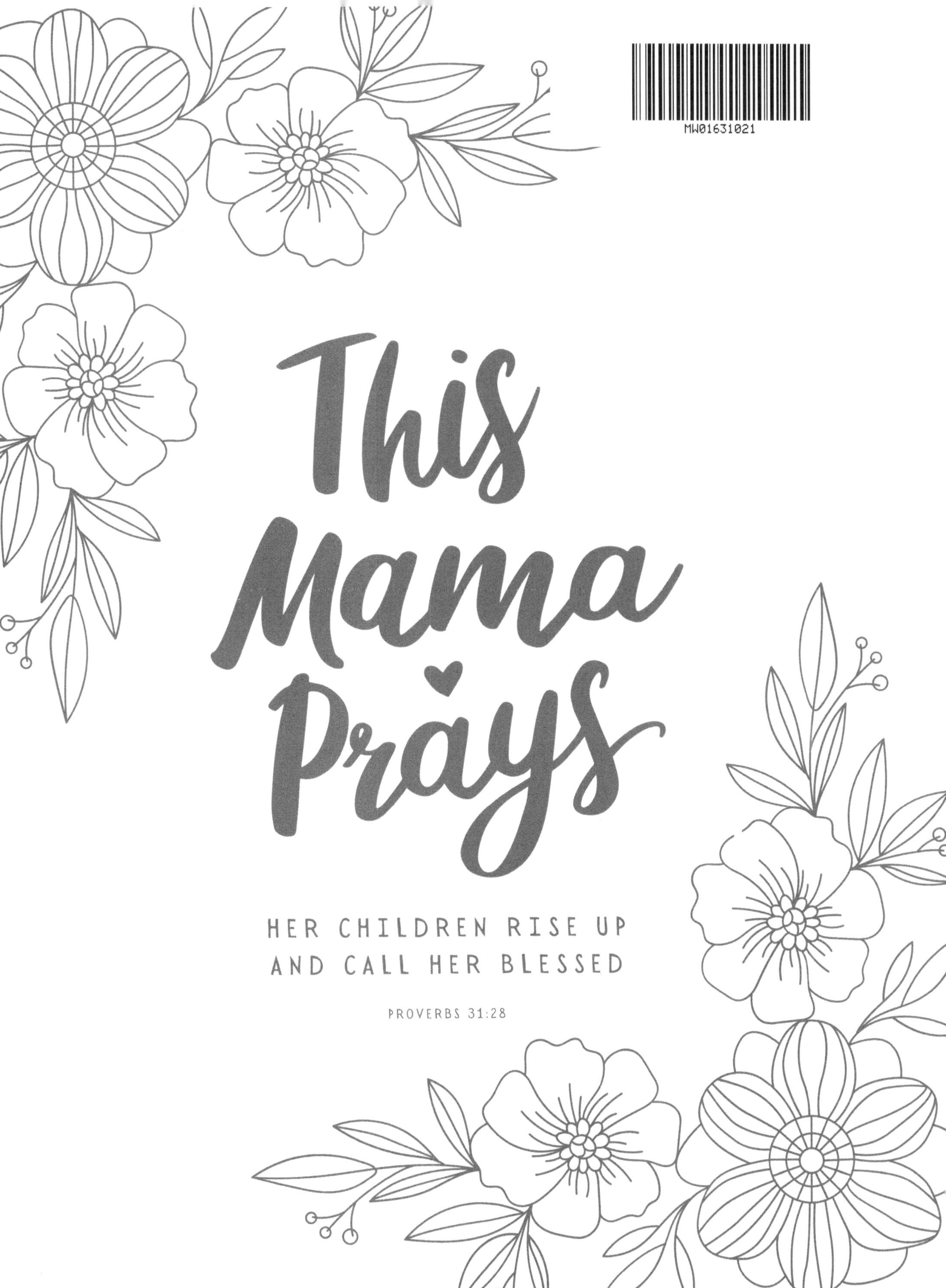

MW01631021
This Mama Prays
HER CHILDREN RISE UP
AND CALL HER BLESSED
PROVERBS 31:28

Her children rise up and call
her blessed...
Many women have done
excellently, but you surpass
them all...

Unless otherwise noted, all Scripture references are provided by The Holy Bible via Bible Gateway, New International Version.

Watercolor artwork by Andra Luta

Published by Skrybe Ltd.

This journal belongs to:

WELCOME, MAMA!

To be a mother is a gift—a gift from God. Motherhood is a path we journey on that is sometimes smooth and sometimes rough. To be a mother is to know strength, to know patience, to know love – to know God.

He is our rock in the midst of the beautiful chaos of parenting. Whether we endure sleepless nights, feel frazzled by endless chores, or feel overwhelmed by busy schedules, He is there in our times of need.

Motherhood is a testament to God's faithfulness, a journey of grace and growth that deepens our relationship with Him. It is a sacred calling and reminds us of the miracle of life and the boundless love of our Heavenly Father.

This journal was created with you, mama, in mind—a sacred space for you to record your prayers, your thoughts and feelings, and your praise for God. Pour out your heart from pen to paper, as you walk the beautiful journey of life and motherhood.

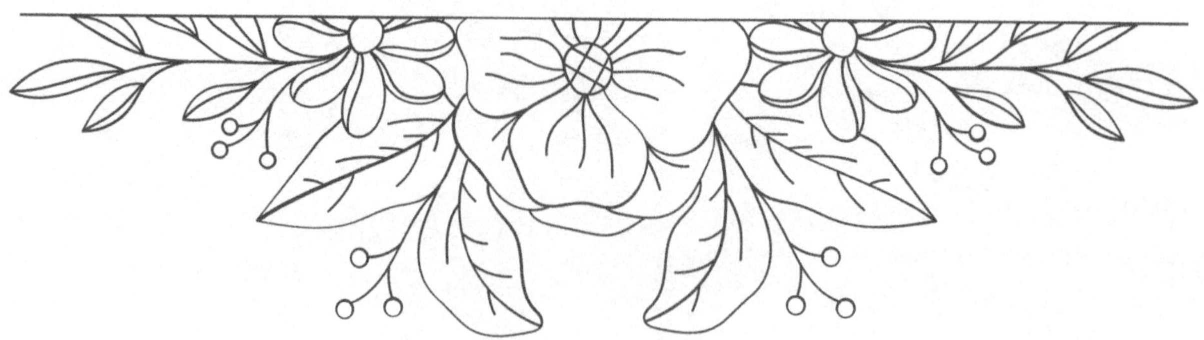

HOW TO USE THIS JOURNAL:

First things first, there is no right or wrong way to use this journal! If you prefer a little structure, simply follow the five guided sections. If you'd like some space to write and explore your thoughts, there are blank lined pages you can run wild with. This journal is yours, and you can choose whatever section calls to you each day.

Every other double page begins with scripture and a prayer promise, providing you with God's word and its application to your life as a mother. If you have feelings weighing heavy on your heart, turn to the 'On my heart' section to document them. And if you are feeling creative—whether that be doodling, sketching or painting—the 'Get creative' section is your very own canvas!

Take inspiration from the daily positive affirmations, read the sweet quotes about motherhood, record your prayers and express your thanks to God. And when He answers your prayers, document them in the designated space, trusting in His timing and reflecting on His love for you.

Remember, God is always with you. Use this prayer journal to deepen your relationship with Him, strengthen your faith, and create a precious book of memories you can look back on and celebrate the wonderful role of motherhood.

But the child's mother said, "As surely as the Lord lives and as you live, I will not leave you."

2 Kings 4:30

Lord, I promise to never leave my child's side, just as You never leave ours. Help me be a steadfast source of love and support in their life.

ON MY HEART TODAY:

GET CREATIVE:

Mothers are like buttons, they hold it all together.

LORD, THANK YOU:

MY PRAISE TO GOD:

I am deserving of love

PRAYER REQUESTS:

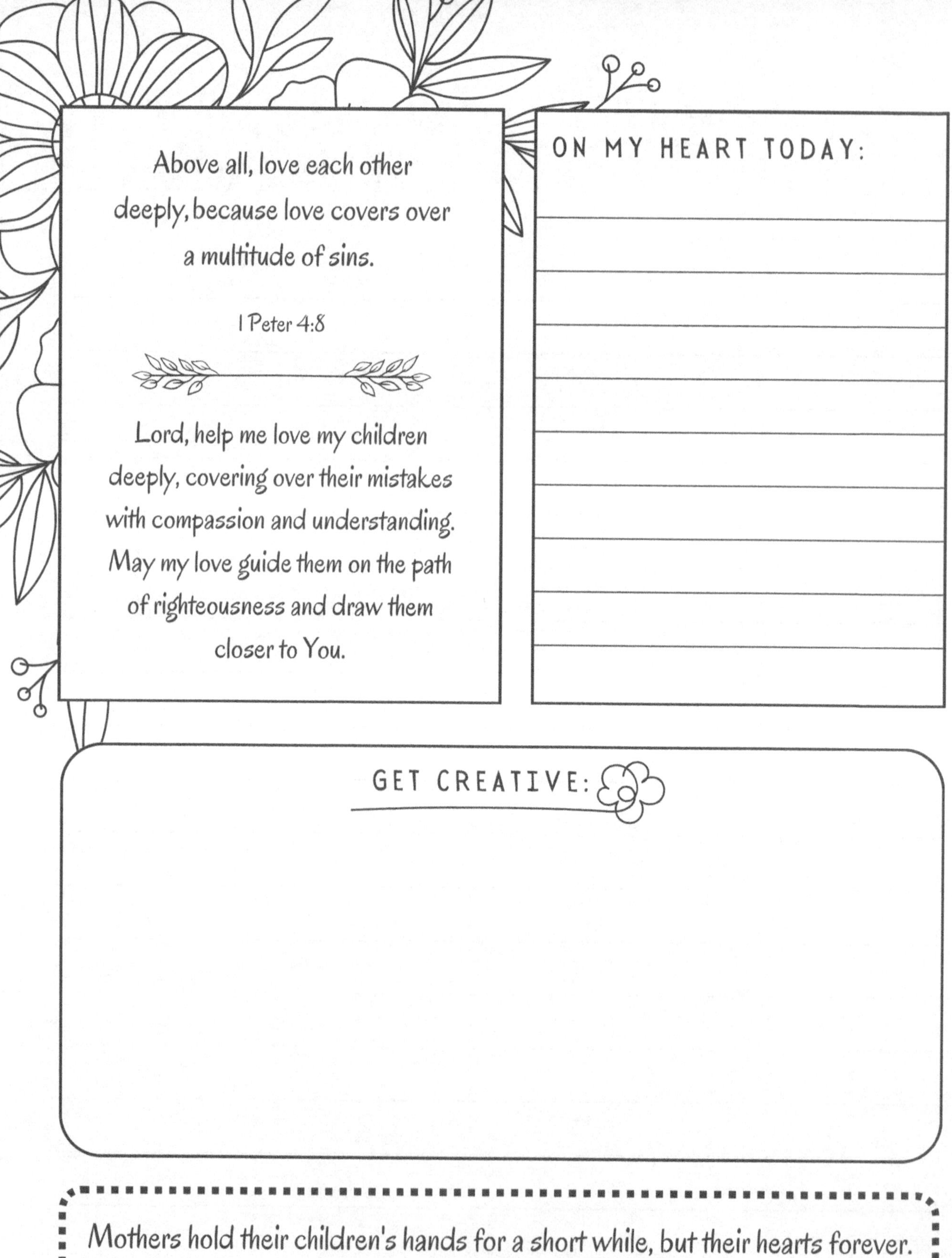

Above all, love each other deeply, because love covers over a multitude of sins.

I Peter 4:8

Lord, help me love my children deeply, covering over their mistakes with compassion and understanding. May my love guide them on the path of righteousness and draw them closer to You.

ON MY HEART TODAY:

GET CREATIVE:

Mothers hold their children's hands for a short while, but their hearts forever.

LORD, THANK YOU:

MY PRAISE TO GOD:

God wants me to be happy

PRAYER REQUESTS:

Cast all your anxiety on Him because he cares for you.

I Peter 5:7

God, as I face my worries, help me to release them into Your loving hands, knowing that You are always there to comfort and guide me.

ON MY HEART TODAY:

GET CREATIVE:

A mother understands what a child does not say.

LORD, THANK YOU:

MY PRAISE TO GOD:

PRAYER REQUESTS:

I embrace each day with positivity

These commandments that I give you today are to be on your hearts. Impress them on your children. Talk about them when you sit at home and when you walk along the road, when you lie down and when you get up.

Deuteronomy 6:6-7

God, may Your commandments guide my actions and shape my words. Help me to instil Your teachings in my children.

ON MY HEART TODAY:

GET CREATIVE:

To the world, you are a mother, but to your family, you are the world.

LORD, THANK YOU:

MY PRAISE TO GOD:

I am a wonderful mother

PRAYER REQUESTS:

Come to me, all you who are weary and burdened, and I will give you rest.

Matthew 11:28

Lord, as I carry the weight of my daily responsibilities as a mother, I turn to You for rest and renewal. Thank You for offering me solace and comfort in moments of weariness.

ON MY HEART TODAY:

GET CREATIVE:

Motherhood: All love begins and ends there.

LORD, THANK YOU:

MY PRAISE TO GOD:

I prioritize my well-being

PRAYER REQUESTS:

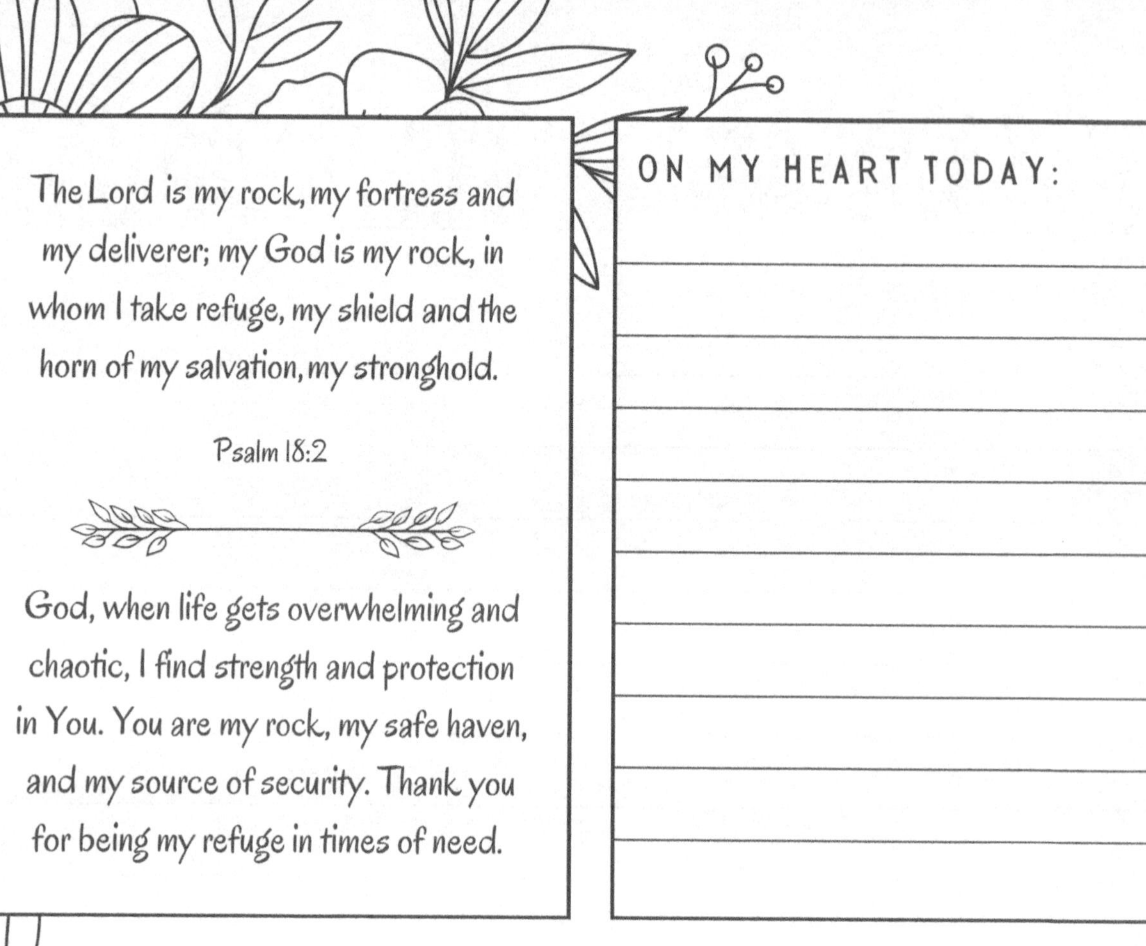

The Lord is my rock, my fortress and my deliverer; my God is my rock, in whom I take refuge, my shield and the horn of my salvation, my stronghold.

Psalm 18:2

God, when life gets overwhelming and chaotic, I find strength and protection in You. You are my rock, my safe haven, and my source of security. Thank you for being my refuge in times of need.

ON MY HEART TODAY:

GET CREATIVE:

A mother's hug lasts long after she lets go.

LORD, THANK YOU:

MY PRAISE TO GOD:

I am more than enough

PRAYER REQUESTS:

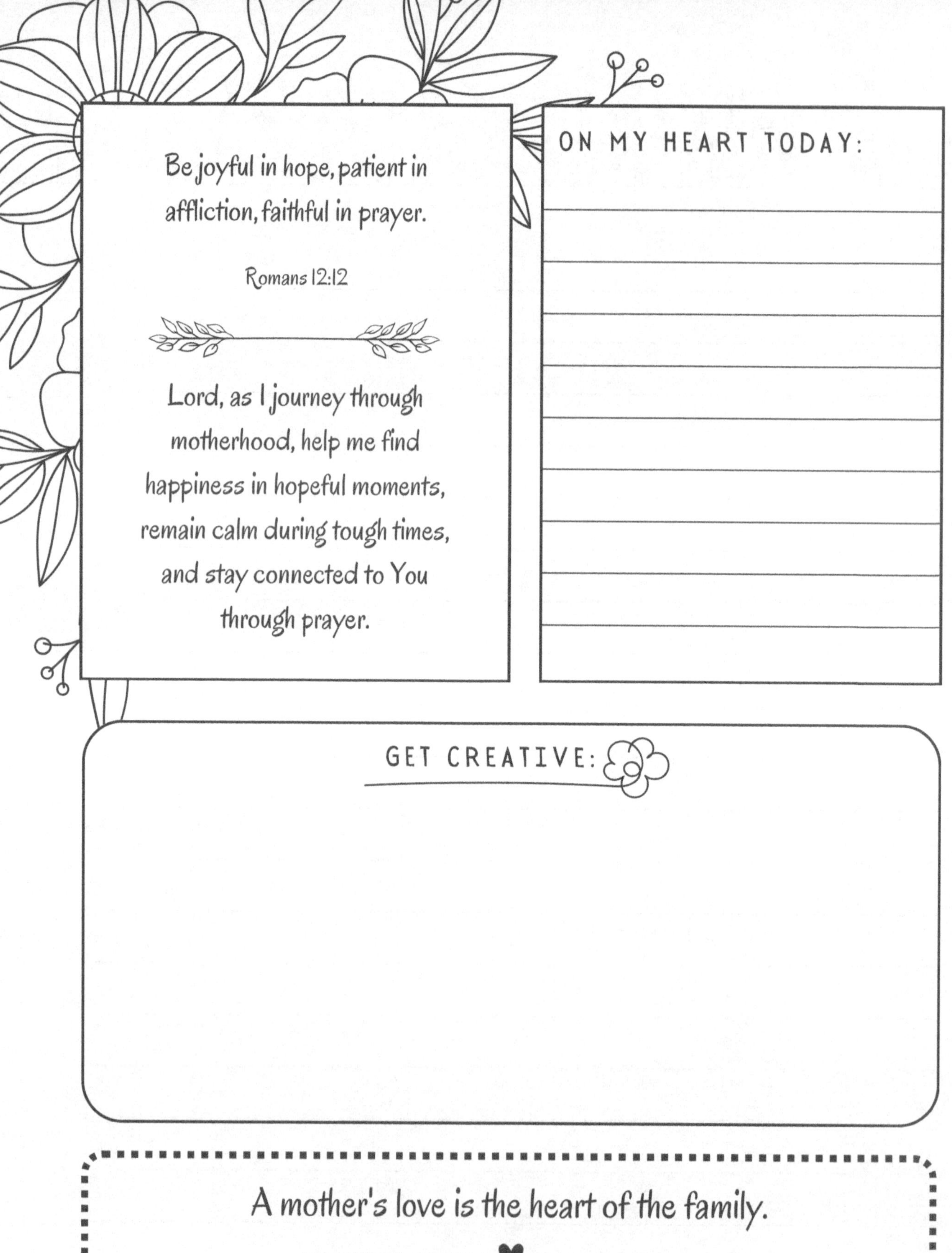

Be joyful in hope, patient in affliction, faithful in prayer.

Romans 12:12

Lord, as I journey through motherhood, help me find happiness in hopeful moments, remain calm during tough times, and stay connected to You through prayer.

ON MY HEART TODAY:

GET CREATIVE:

A mother's love is the heart of the family.

LORD, THANK YOU:

MY PRAISE TO GOD:

I believe in myself

PRAYER REQUESTS:

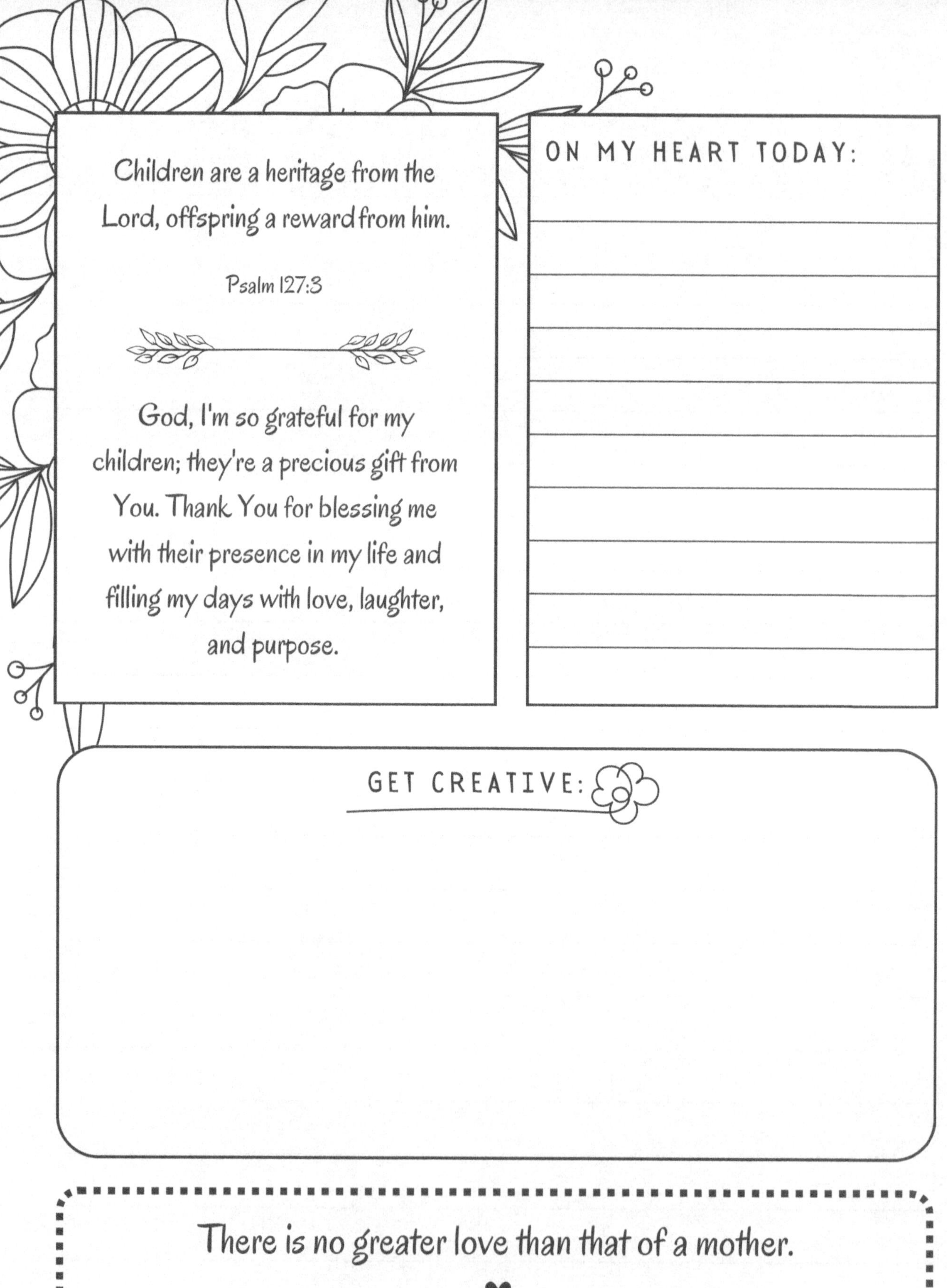

Children are a heritage from the Lord, offspring a reward from him.

Psalm 127:3

God, I'm so grateful for my children; they're a precious gift from You. Thank You for blessing me with their presence in my life and filling my days with love, laughter, and purpose.

ON MY HEART TODAY:

GET CREATIVE:

There is no greater love than that of a mother.

LORD, THANK YOU:

MY PRAISE TO GOD:

I greet each day with gratitude

PRAYER REQUESTS:

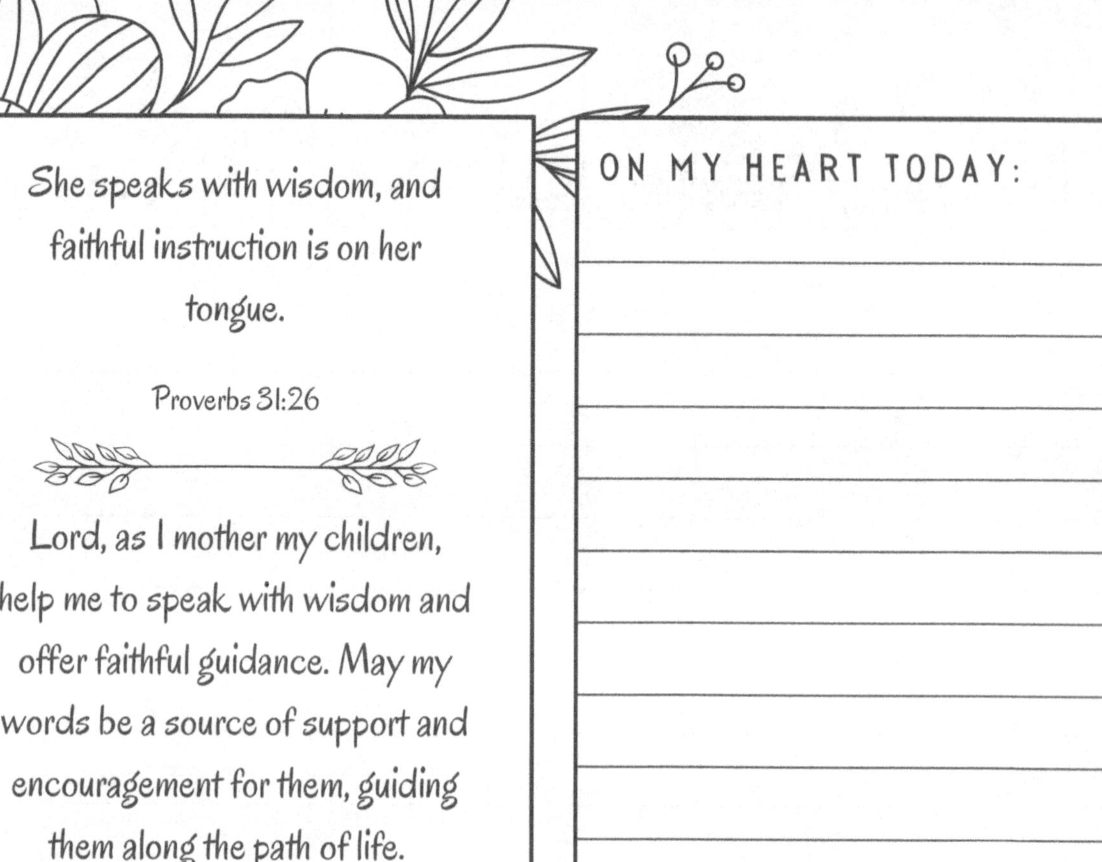

She speaks with wisdom, and faithful instruction is on her tongue.

Proverbs 31:26

Lord, as I mother my children, help me to speak with wisdom and offer faithful guidance. May my words be a source of support and encouragement for them, guiding them along the path of life.

ON MY HEART TODAY:

GET CREATIVE:

Life doesn't come with a manual, it comes with a mother.

LORD, THANK YOU:

MY PRAISE TO GOD:

My challenges help me grow

PRAYER REQUESTS:

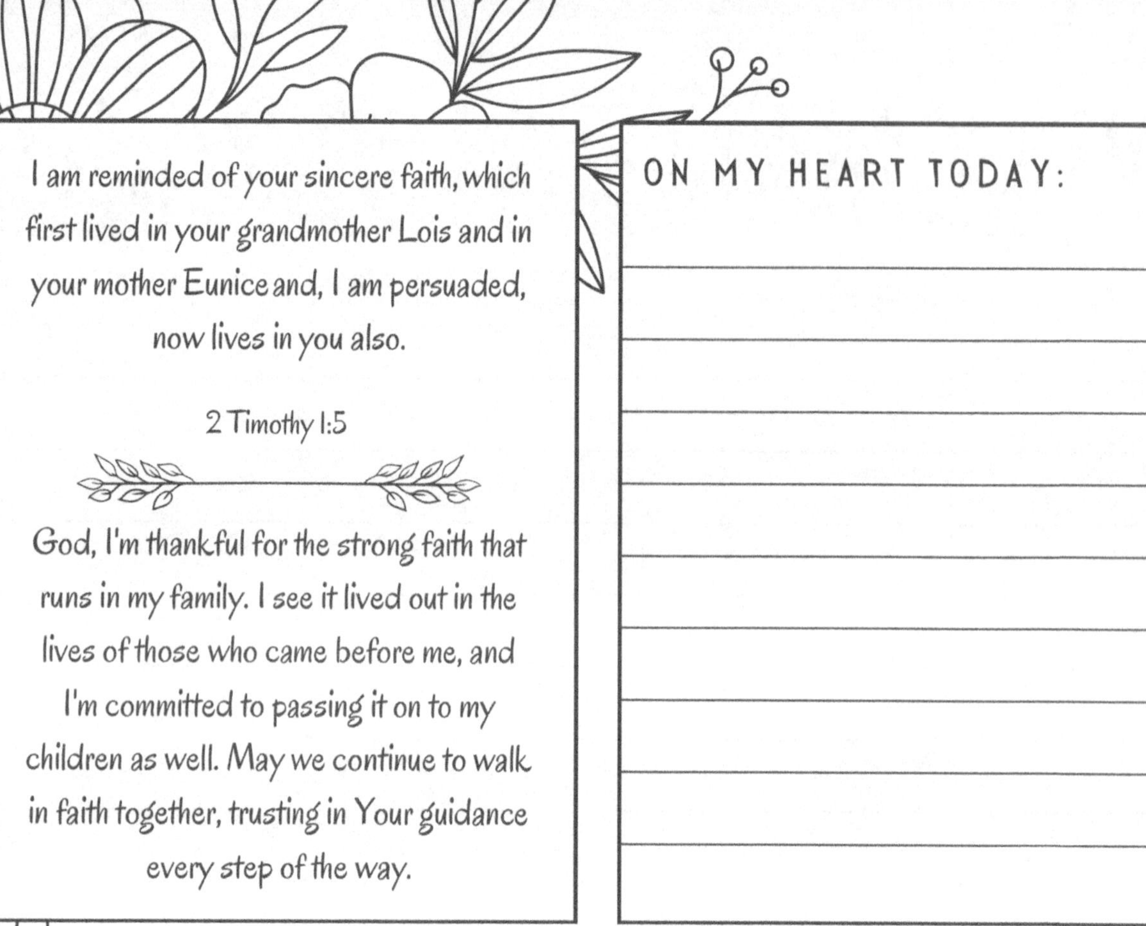

I am reminded of your sincere faith, which first lived in your grandmother Lois and in your mother Eunice and, I am persuaded, now lives in you also.

2 Timothy 1:5

God, I'm thankful for the strong faith that runs in my family. I see it lived out in the lives of those who came before me, and I'm committed to passing it on to my children as well. May we continue to walk in faith together, trusting in Your guidance every step of the way.

ON MY HEART TODAY:

GET CREATIVE:

Family is where life begins and love never ends.

LORD, THANK YOU:

MY PRAISE TO GOD:

Today is going to be a great day

PRAYER REQUESTS:

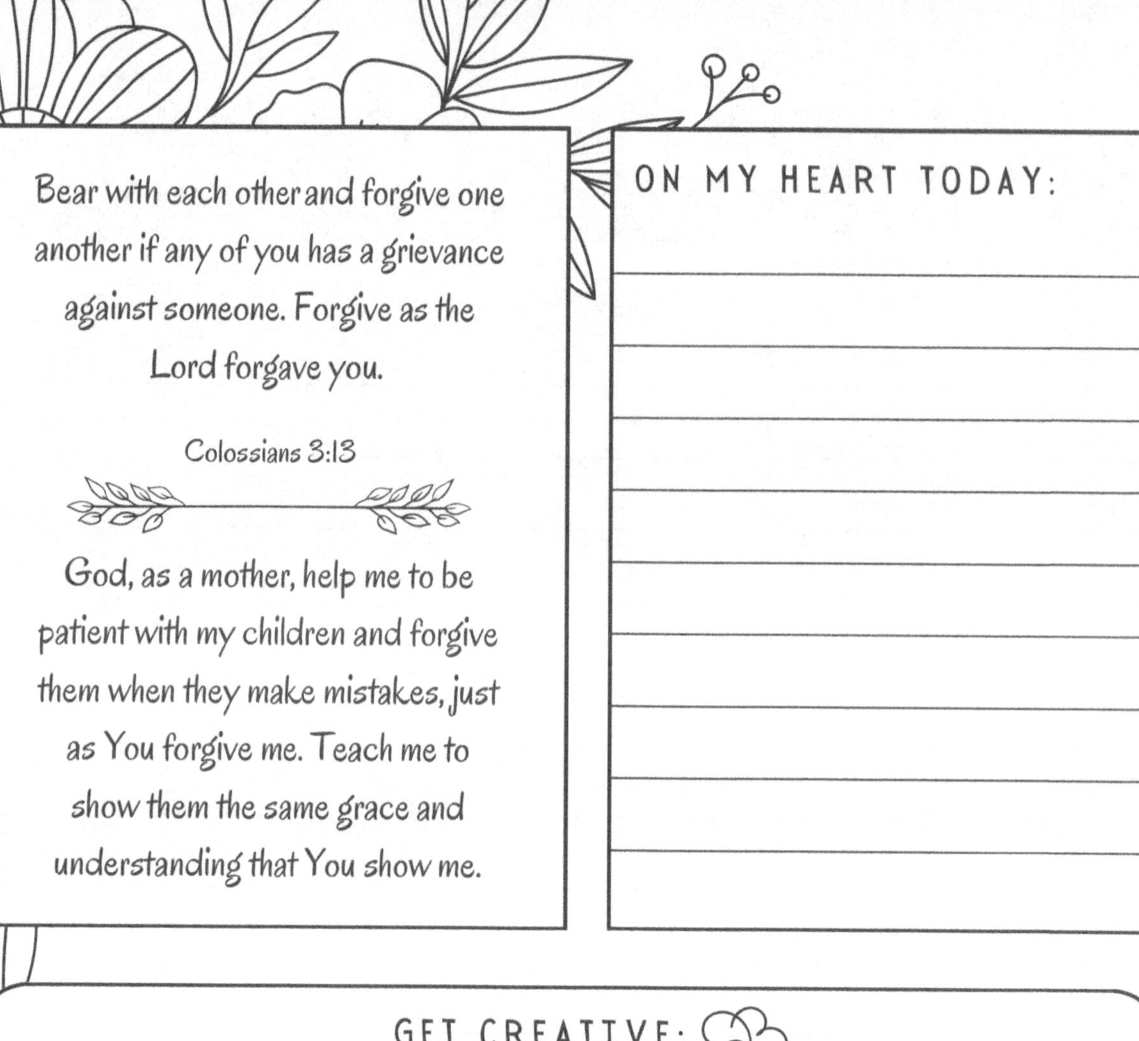

Bear with each other and forgive one another if any of you has a grievance against someone. Forgive as the Lord forgave you.

Colossians 3:13

God, as a mother, help me to be patient with my children and forgive them when they make mistakes, just as You forgive me. Teach me to show them the same grace and understanding that You show me.

ON MY HEART TODAY:

GET CREATIVE:

Mom, a title just above queen.

LORD, THANK YOU:

MY PRAISE TO GOD:

Let your light shine

PRAYER REQUESTS:

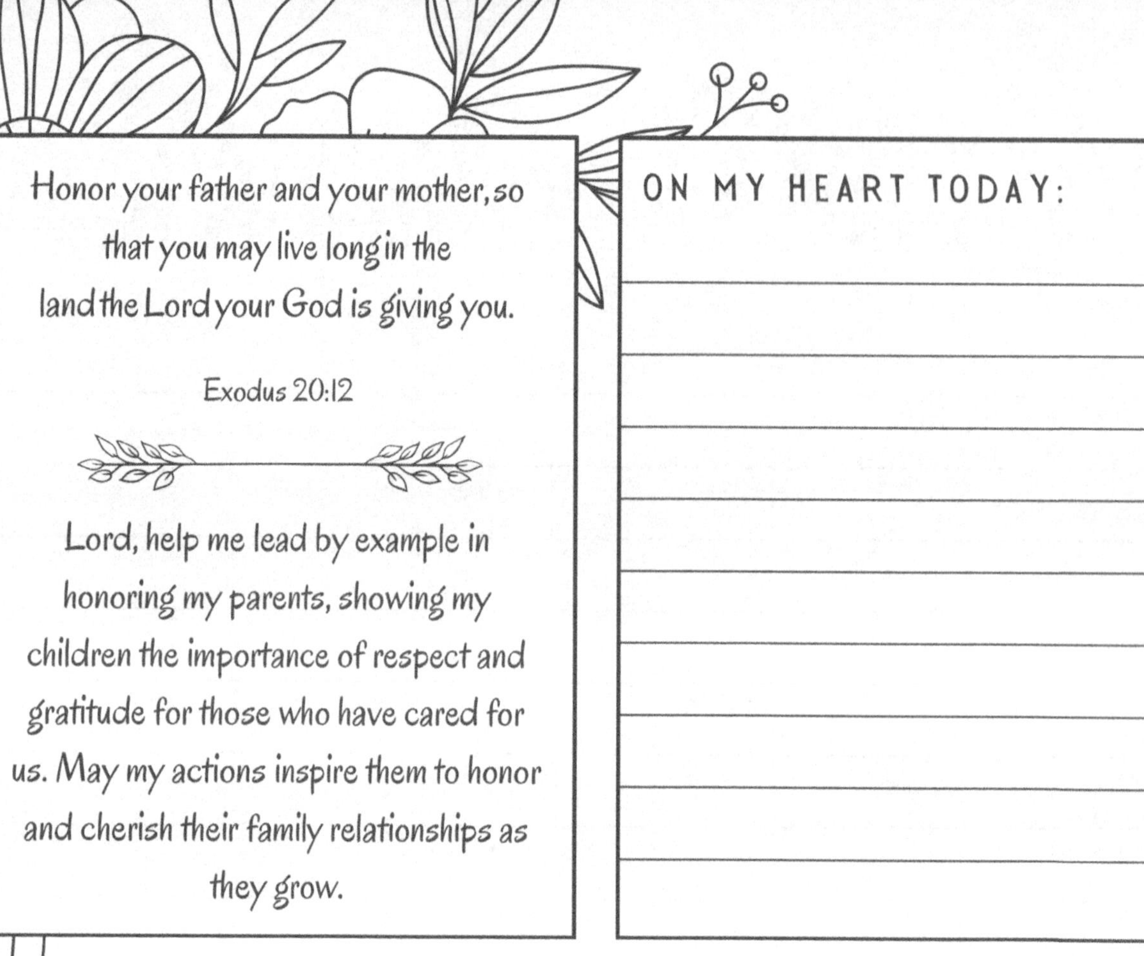

Honor your father and your mother, so that you may live long in the land the Lord your God is giving you.

Exodus 20:12

Lord, help me lead by example in honoring my parents, showing my children the importance of respect and gratitude for those who have cared for us. May my actions inspire them to honor and cherish their family relationships as they grow.

ON MY HEART TODAY:

GET CREATIVE:

Family is not an important thing. It's everything.

LORD, THANK YOU:

MY PRAISE TO GOD:

I can make a difference

PRAYER REQUESTS:

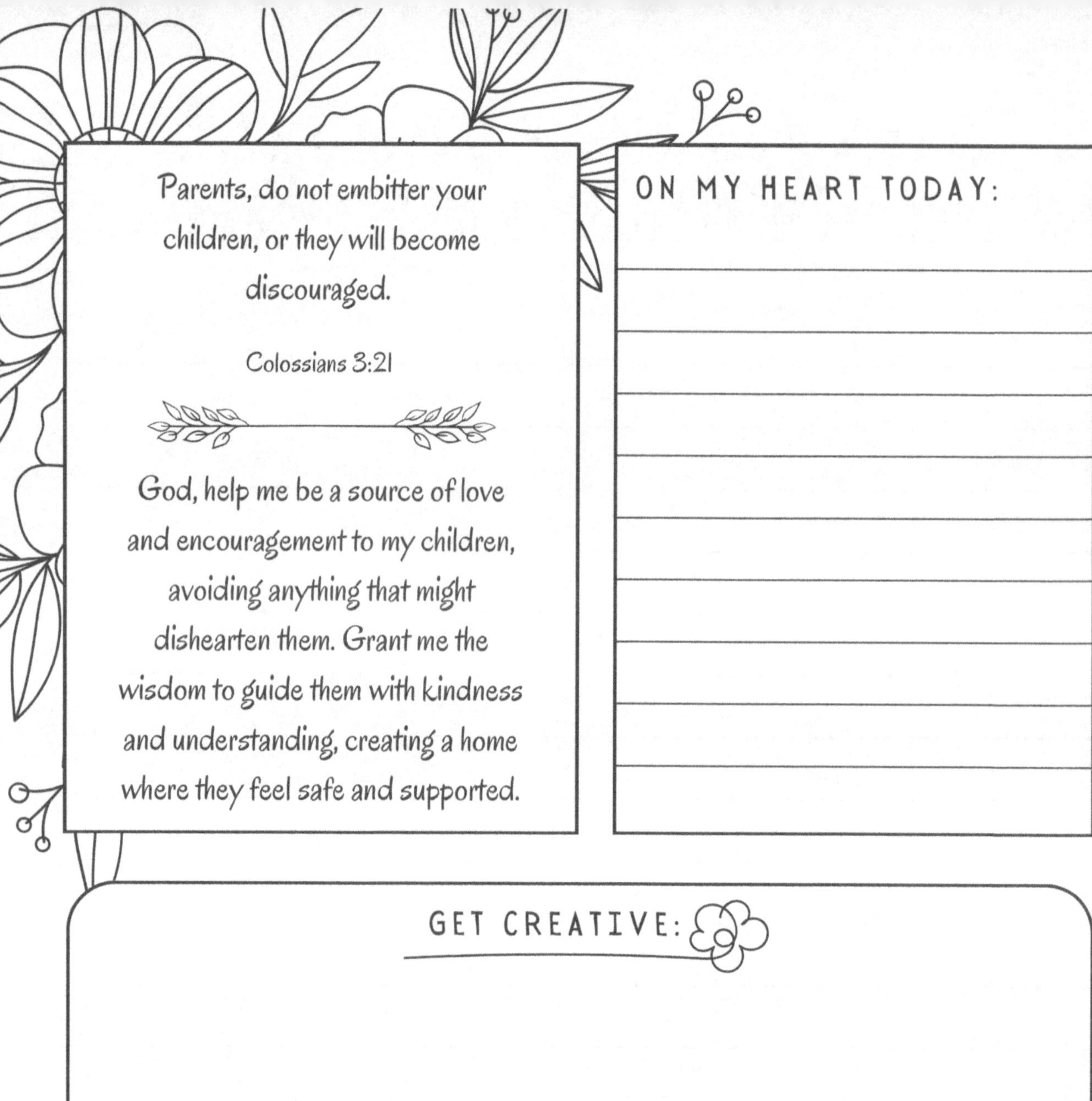

Parents, do not embitter your children, or they will become discouraged.

Colossians 3:21

God, help me be a source of love and encouragement to my children, avoiding anything that might dishearten them. Grant me the wisdom to guide them with kindness and understanding, creating a home where they feel safe and supported.

ON MY HEART TODAY:

GET CREATIVE:

Mom life is the best life.

LORD, THANK YOU:

MY PRAISE TO GOD:

PRAYER REQUESTS:

I am proud of myself

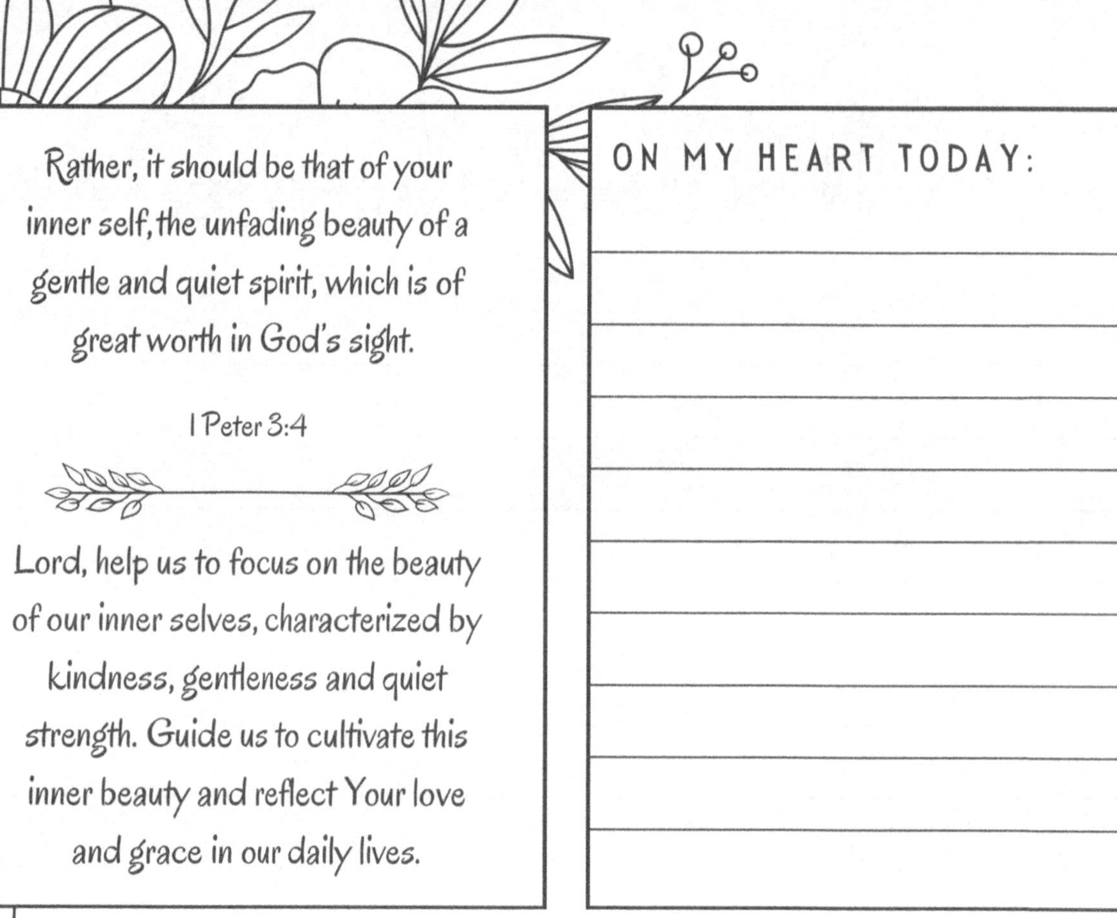

Rather, it should be that of your inner self, the unfading beauty of a gentle and quiet spirit, which is of great worth in God's sight.

1 Peter 3:4

Lord, help us to focus on the beauty of our inner selves, characterized by kindness, gentleness and quiet strength. Guide us to cultivate this inner beauty and reflect Your love and grace in our daily lives.

ON MY HEART TODAY:

GET CREATIVE:

Never forget the difference you've made.

LORD, THANK YOU:

MY PRAISE TO GOD:

PRAYER REQUESTS:

I am in tune with this moment

A woman giving birth to a child has pain because her time has come; but when her baby is born she forgets the anguish because of her joy that a child is born into the world.

John 16:21

God, help us to remember that even in difficult times, there is always hope for a brighter future. Give us the strength to endure challenges, knowing that they will lead to moments of immense happiness and fulfilment.

ON MY HEART TODAY:

GET CREATIVE:

Family is the anchor that holds us through life's storms.

LORD, THANK YOU:

MY PRAISE TO GOD:

I can do hard things

PRAYER REQUESTS:

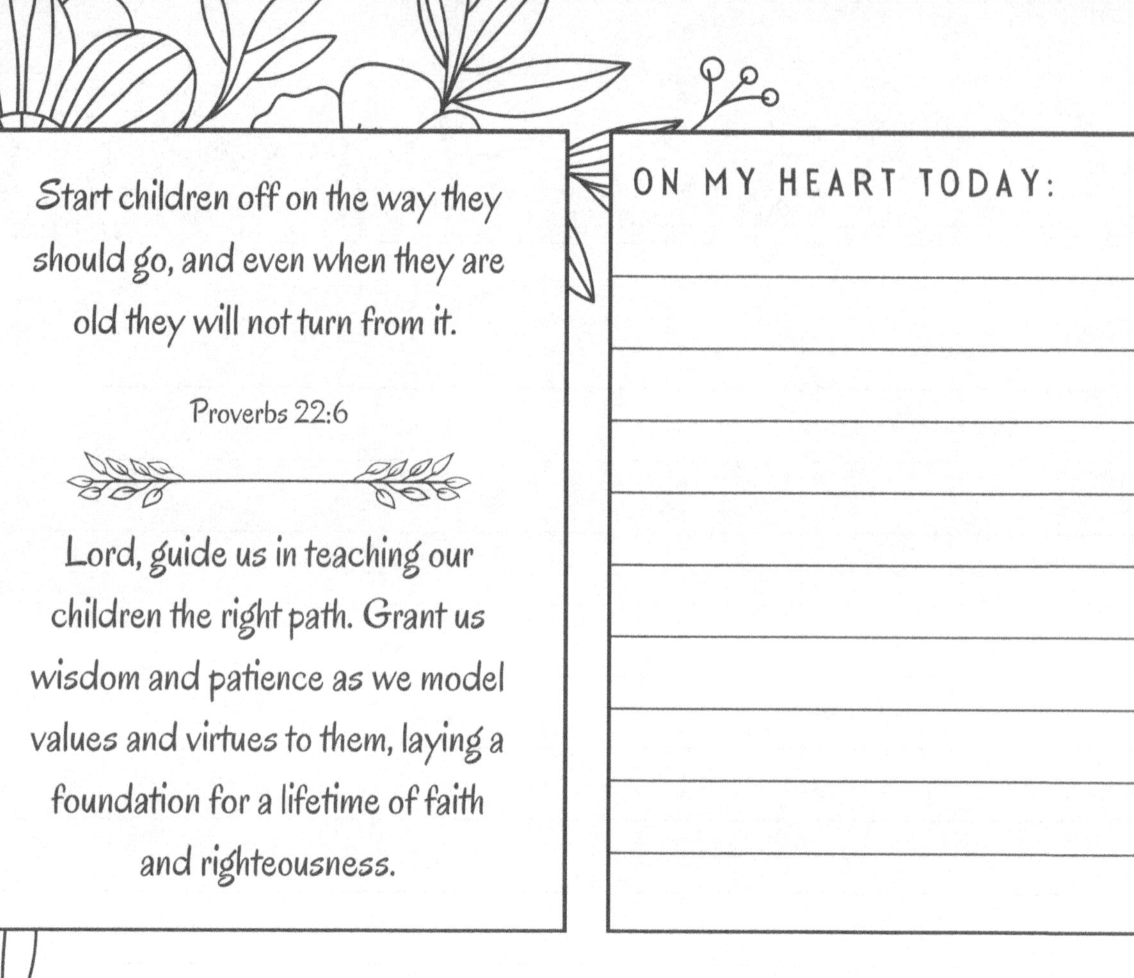

Start children off on the way they should go, and even when they are old they will not turn from it.

Proverbs 22:6

Lord, guide us in teaching our children the right path. Grant us wisdom and patience as we model values and virtues to them, laying a foundation for a lifetime of faith and righteousness.

ON MY HEART TODAY:

GET CREATIVE:

My greatest blessings call me mom.

LORD, THANK YOU:

MY PRAISE TO GOD:

Life is good

PRAYER REQUESTS:

God is within her, she will not fall;
God will help her at break of day.

Psalm 46:5

Lord, knowing You're with me gives me strength. I won't be shaken, and I'll face each day with confidence, resilience and determination.

ON MY HEART TODAY:

GET CREATIVE:

A mother is your first friend, your best friend, your forever friend.

LORD, THANK YOU:

MY PRAISE TO GOD:

My feelings are valid

PRAYER REQUESTS:

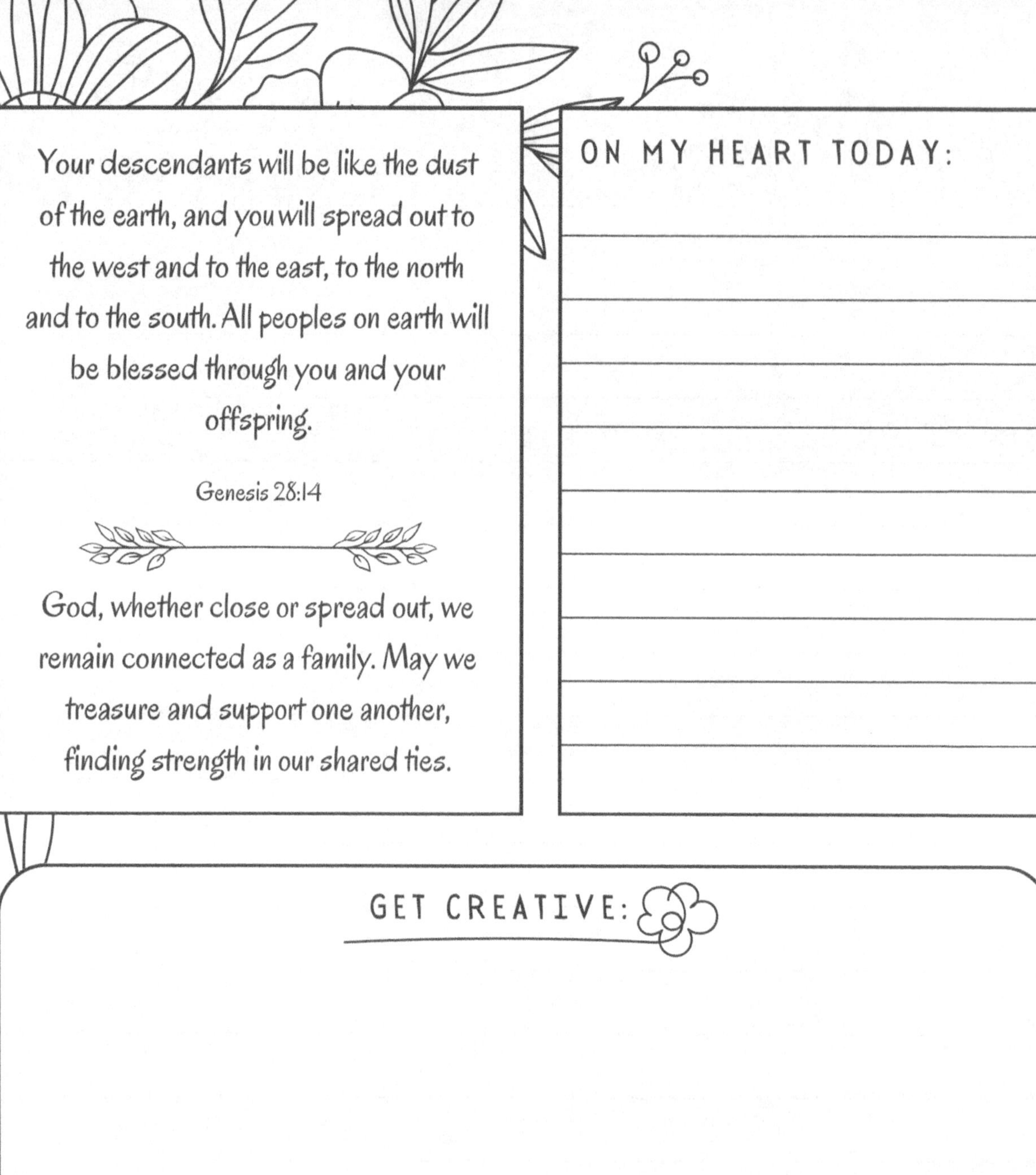

Your descendants will be like the dust of the earth, and you will spread out to the west and to the east, to the north and to the south. All peoples on earth will be blessed through you and your offspring.

Genesis 28:14

God, whether close or spread out, we remain connected as a family. May we treasure and support one another, finding strength in our shared ties.

ON MY HEART TODAY:

GET CREATIVE:

Our family is a circle of strength and love.

LORD, THANK YOU:

MY PRAISE TO GOD:

I am a beautiful creation

PRAYER REQUESTS:

I have no greater joy than to hear that my children are walking in the truth.

3 John 1:4

Lord, as a mother, my greatest joy is to see my children following Your path. May they find fulfilment and purpose, bringing joy to my heart and glory to Your name.

ON MY HEART TODAY:

GET CREATIVE:

A mother is always the beginning. She is how things begin.

LORD, THANK YOU:

MY PRAISE TO GOD:

I am faithful

PRAYER REQUESTS:

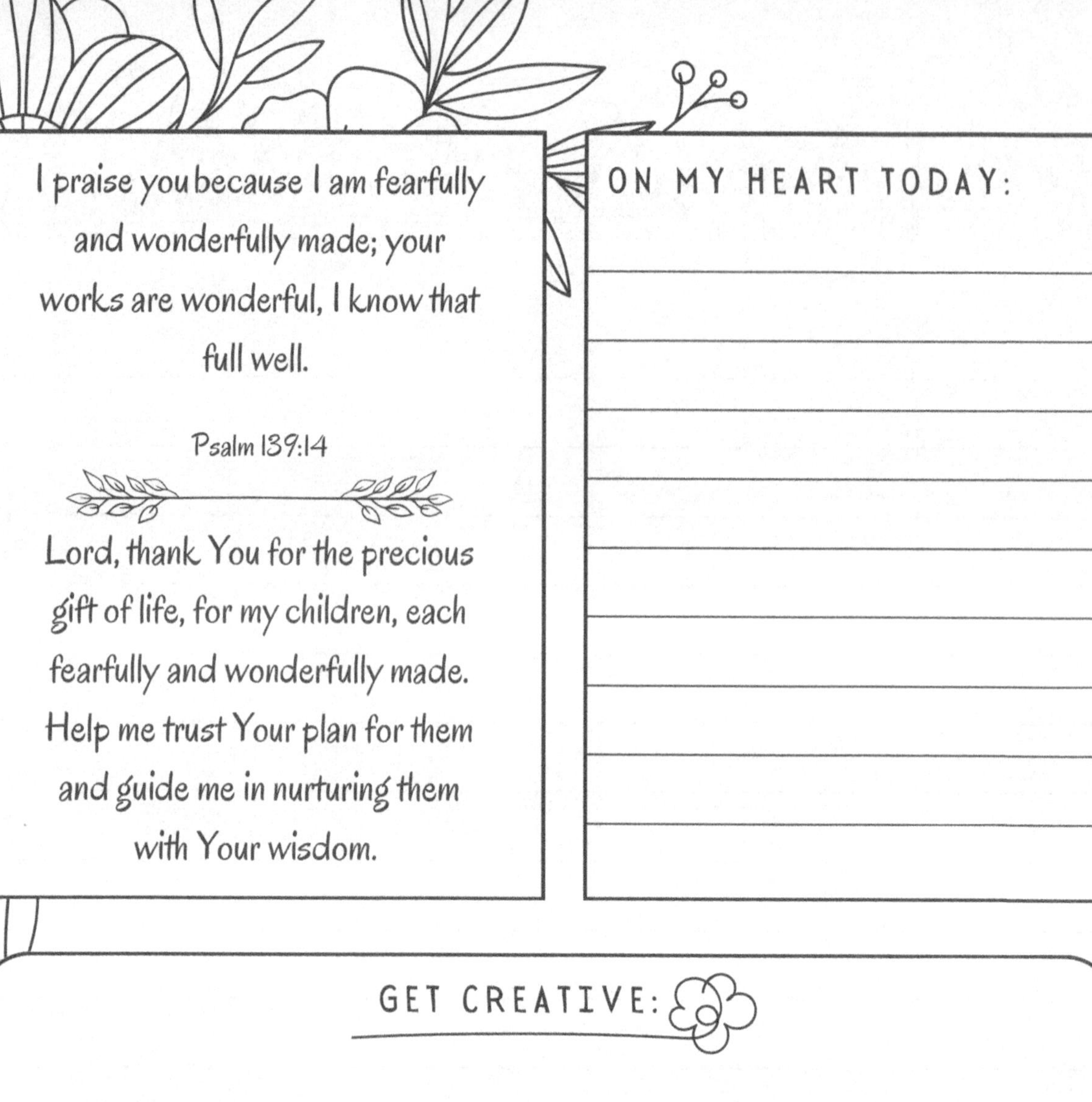

I praise you because I am fearfully and wonderfully made; your works are wonderful, I know that full well.

Psalm 139:14

Lord, thank You for the precious gift of life, for my children, each fearfully and wonderfully made. Help me trust Your plan for them and guide me in nurturing them with Your wisdom.

ON MY HEART TODAY:

GET CREATIVE:

A mother is like a flower, each one beautiful and unique.

LORD, THANK YOU:

MY PRAISE TO GOD:

God will never leave me

PRAYER REQUESTS:

Those who hope in the Lord will renew their strength. They will soar on wings like eagles; they will run and not grow weary, they will walk and not be faint.

Isaiah 40:31

God, as we trust in You, renew our strength. Help us wait on You with patience, knowing You alone can sustain us. Strengthen our faith to endure challenges without growing weary.

ON MY HEART TODAY:

GET CREATIVE:

The days are long, but the years are short.

LORD, THANK YOU:

MY PRAISE TO GOD:

I will dedicate time to myself

PRAYER REQUESTS:

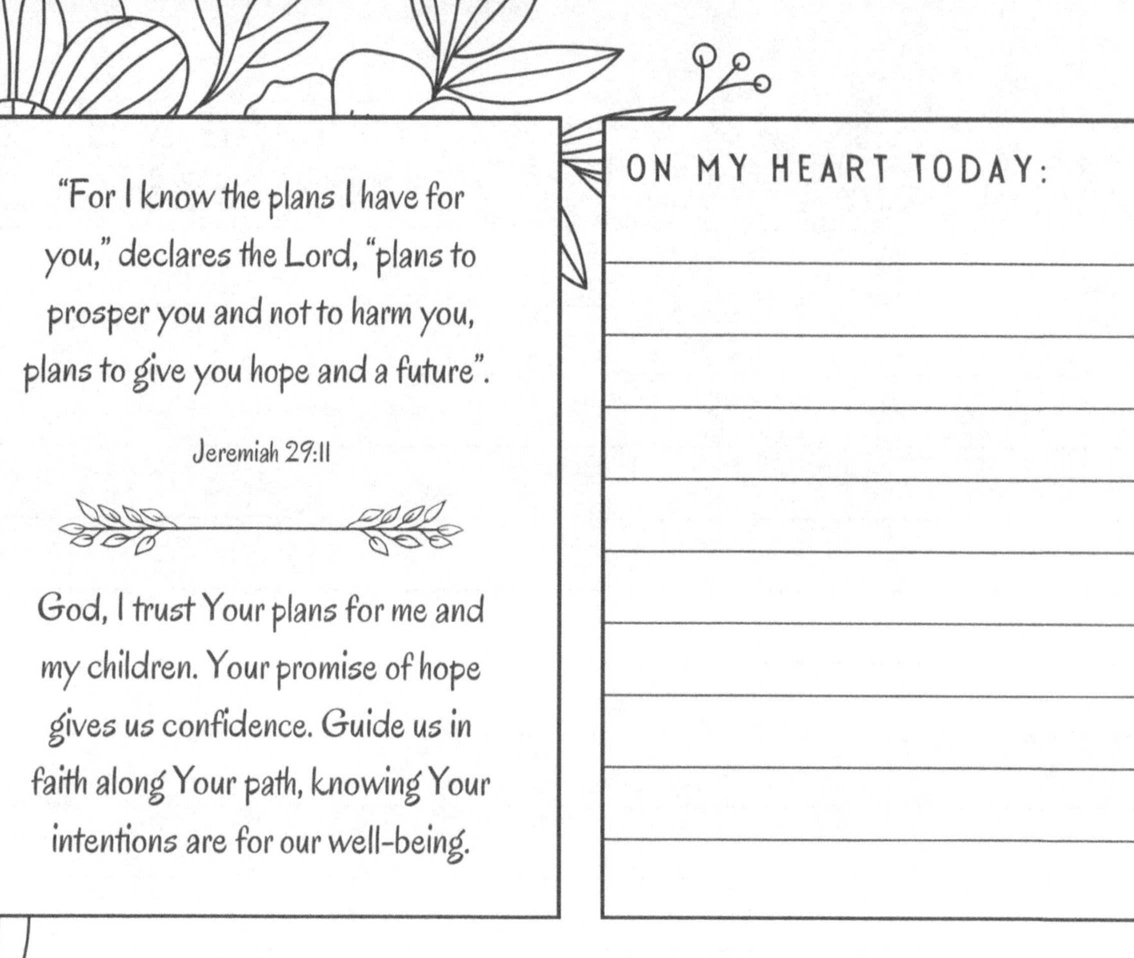

"For I know the plans I have for you," declares the Lord, "plans to prosper you and not to harm you, plans to give you hope and a future".

Jeremiah 29:11

God, I trust Your plans for me and my children. Your promise of hope gives us confidence. Guide us in faith along Your path, knowing Your intentions are for our well-being.

ON MY HEART TODAY:

GET CREATIVE:

Mom's love knows no bounds.

LORD, THANK YOU:

MY PRAISE TO GOD:

PRAYER REQUESTS:

My future is bright

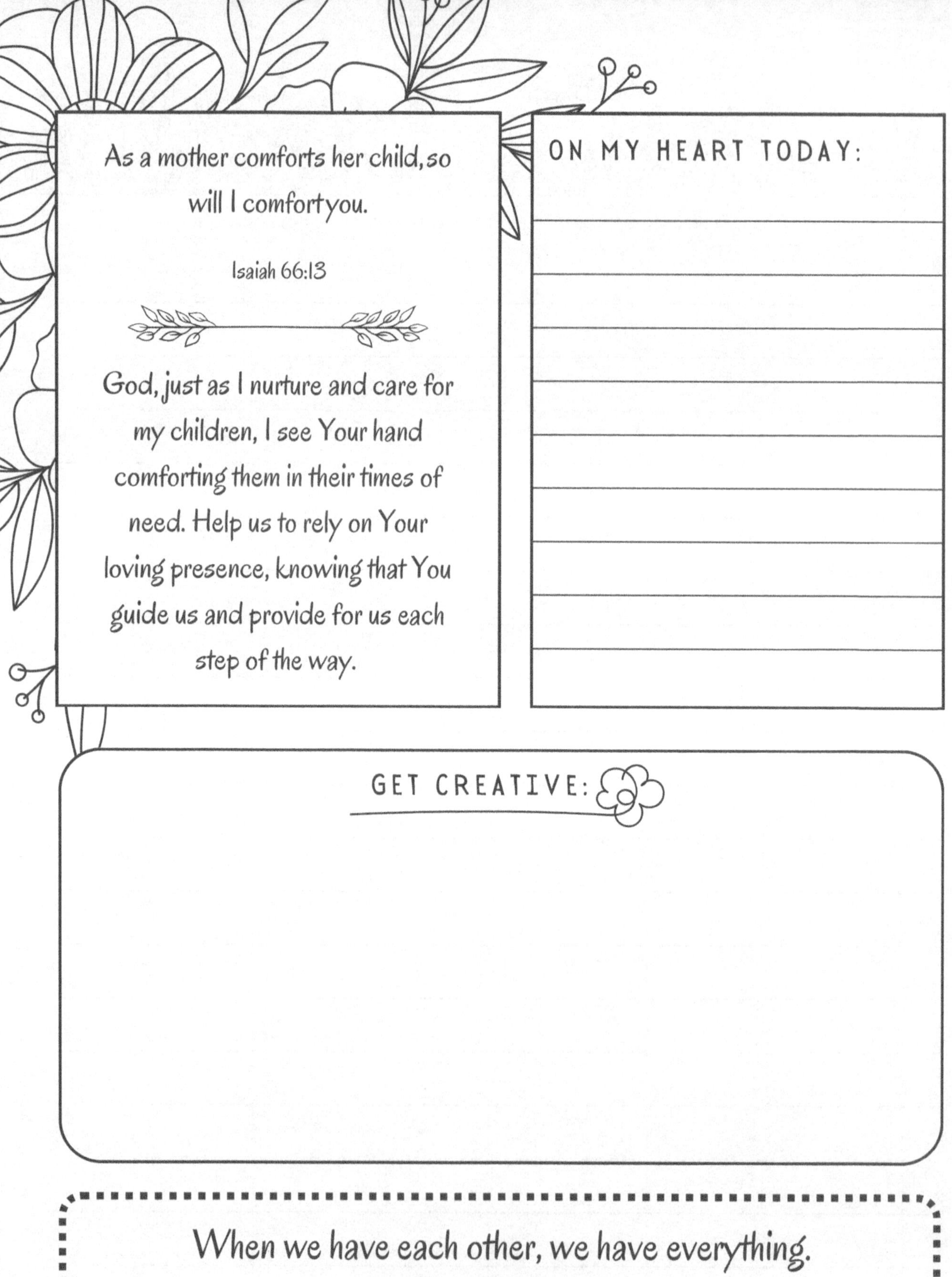

As a mother comforts her child, so will I comfort you.

Isaiah 66:13

God, just as I nurture and care for my children, I see Your hand comforting them in their times of need. Help us to rely on Your loving presence, knowing that You guide us and provide for us each step of the way.

ON MY HEART TODAY:

GET CREATIVE:

When we have each other, we have everything.

LORD, THANK YOU:

MY PRAISE TO GOD:

I am determined

PRAYER REQUESTS:

Be strong and courageous. Do not be afraid; do not be discouraged, for the Lord your God will be with you wherever you go.

Joshua 1:9

Lord, we are grateful that You will never leave us nor forsake us. Grant us the courage to face the challenges ahead, knowing that You are with us always.

ON MY HEART TODAY:

GET CREATIVE:

The most precious jewels you'll ever have around your neck are the arms of your children.

LORD, THANK YOU:

MY PRAISE TO GOD:

Everything I need is within me

PRAYER REQUESTS:

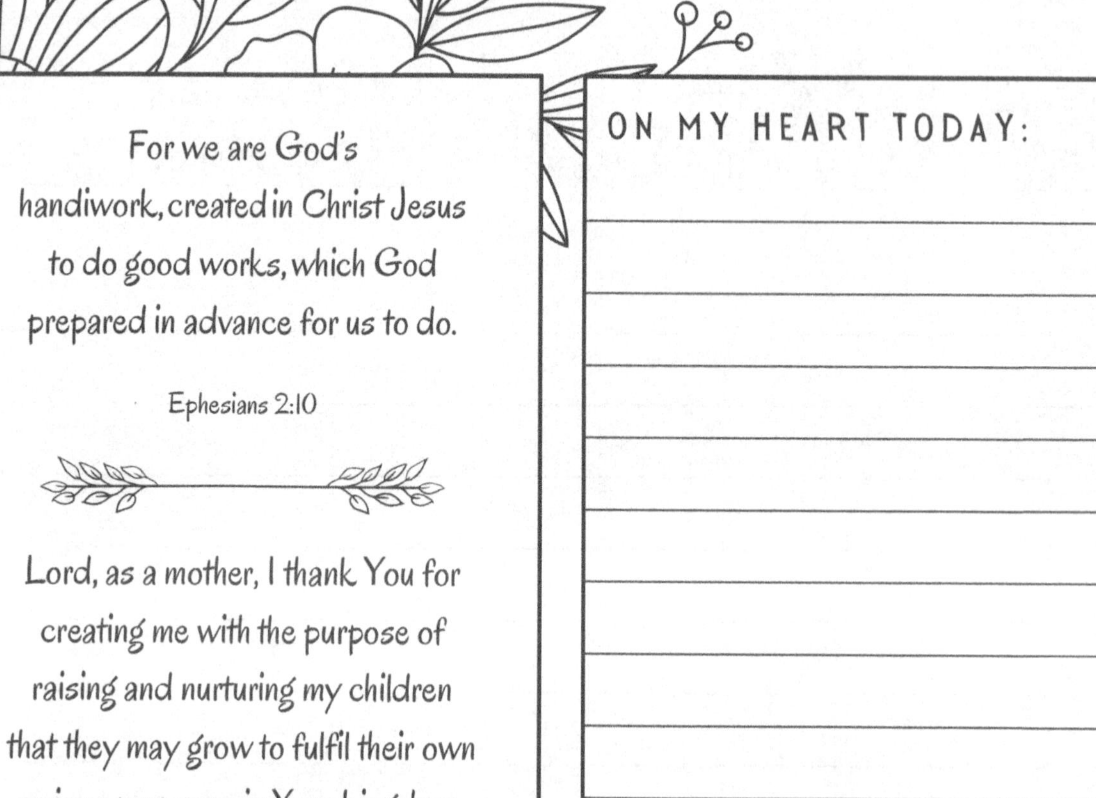

For we are God's handiwork, created in Christ Jesus to do good works, which God prepared in advance for us to do.

Ephesians 2:10

Lord, as a mother, I thank You for creating me with the purpose of raising and nurturing my children that they may grow to fulfil their own unique purposes in Your kingdom.

ON MY HEART TODAY:

GET CREATIVE:

Motherhood is love in its purest form.

LORD, THANK YOU:

MY PRAISE TO GOD:

I recognize my self-worth

PRAYER REQUESTS:

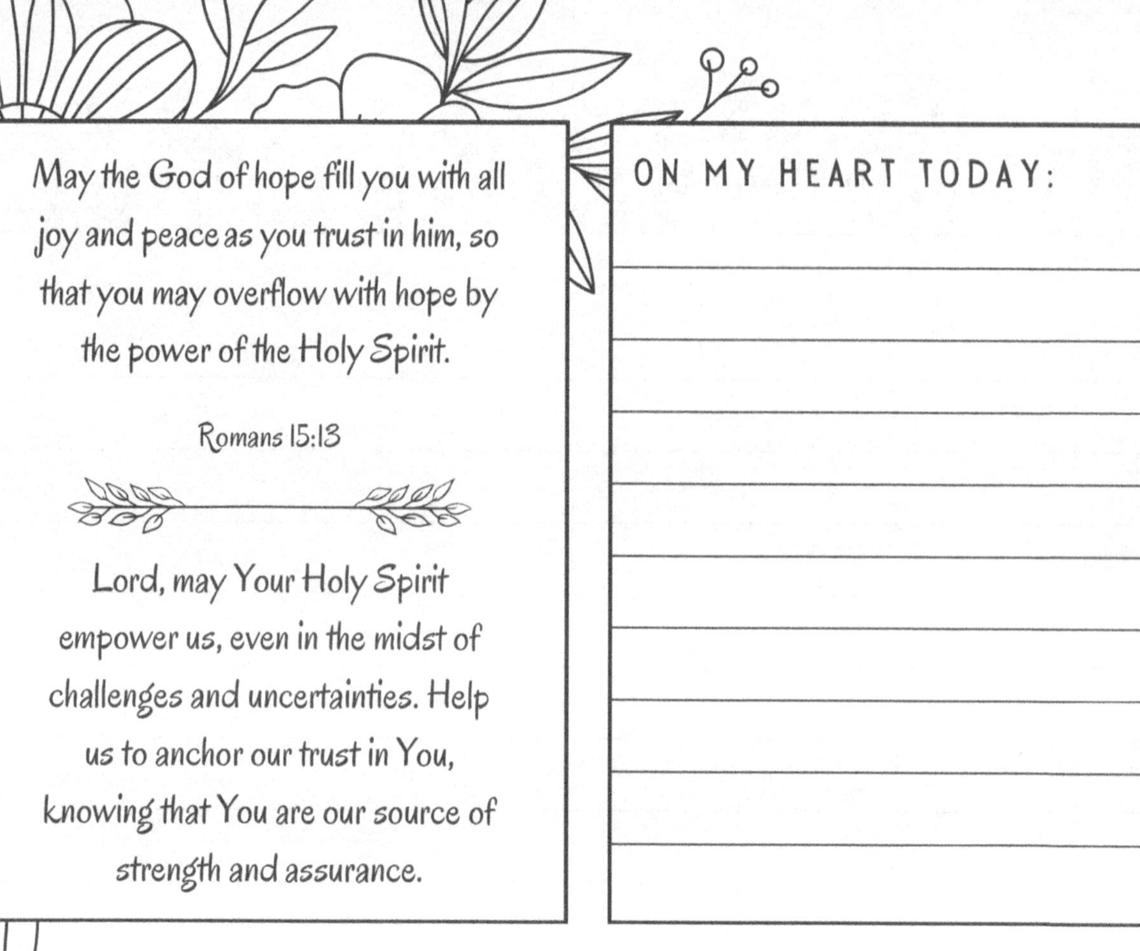

May the God of hope fill you with all joy and peace as you trust in him, so that you may overflow with hope by the power of the Holy Spirit.

Romans 15:13

Lord, may Your Holy Spirit empower us, even in the midst of challenges and uncertainties. Help us to anchor our trust in You, knowing that You are our source of strength and assurance.

ON MY HEART TODAY:

GET CREATIVE:

The most important time is family time.

LORD, THANK YOU:

MY PRAISE TO GOD:

PRAYER REQUESTS:

I trust in God's timing

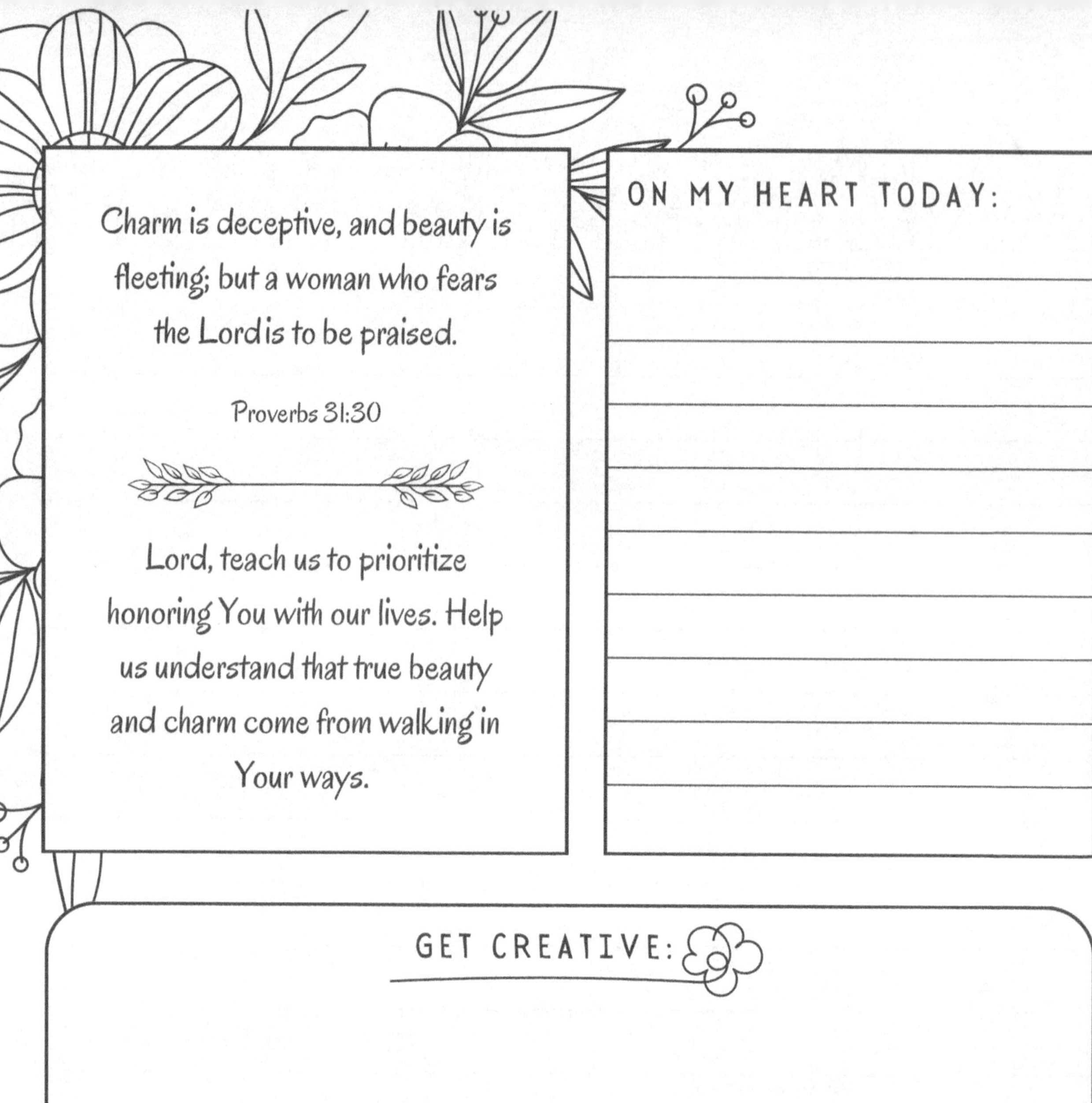

Charm is deceptive, and beauty is fleeting; but a woman who fears the Lord is to be praised.

Proverbs 31:30

Lord, teach us to prioritize honoring You with our lives. Help us understand that true beauty and charm come from walking in Your ways.

ON MY HEART TODAY:

GET CREATIVE:

There's no way to be a perfect mother and a million ways to be a good one.

LORD, THANK YOU:

MY PRAISE TO GOD:

I am loved by God just as I am

PRAYER REQUESTS:

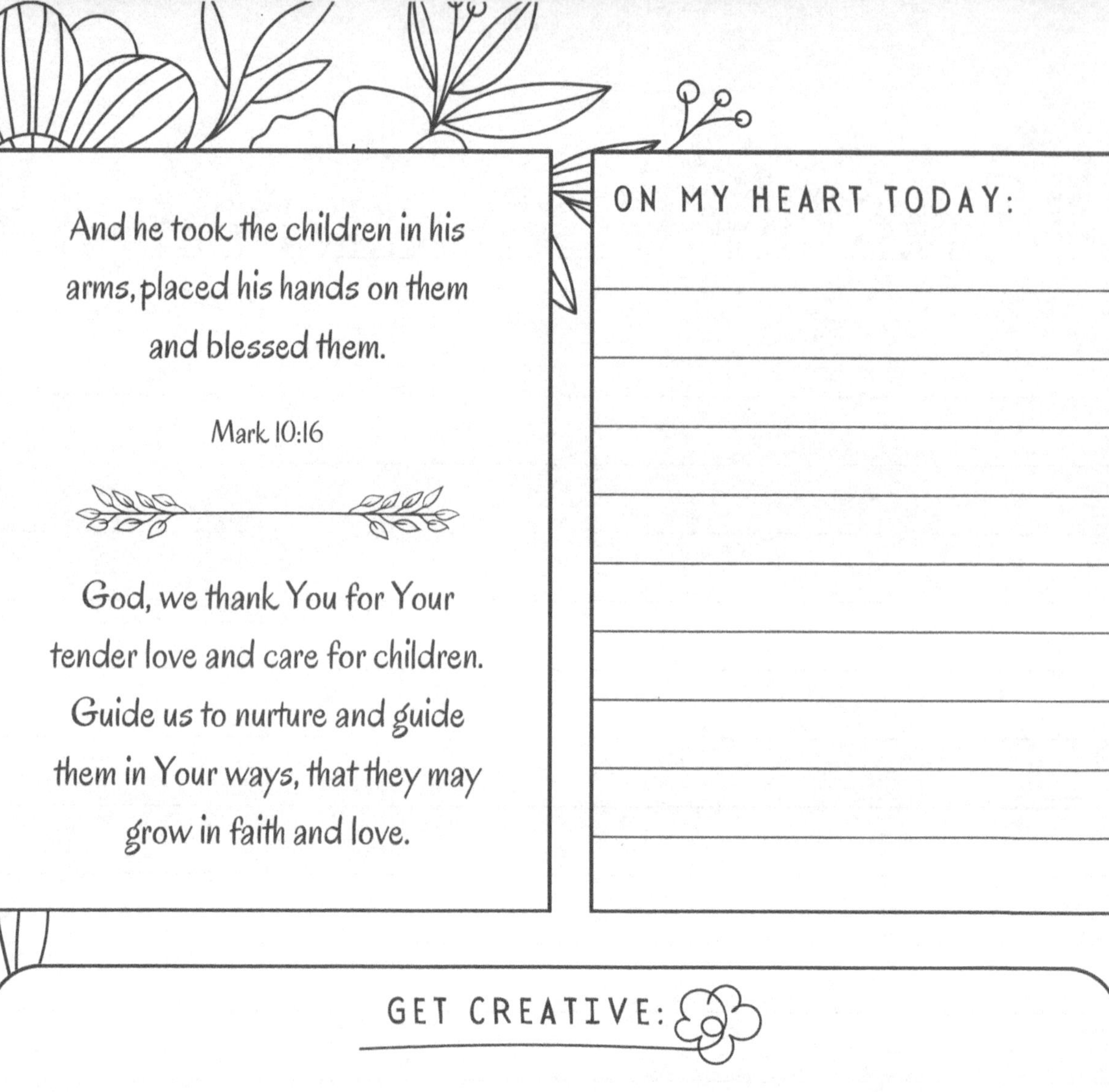

And he took the children in his arms, placed his hands on them and blessed them.

Mark 10:16

God, we thank You for Your tender love and care for children. Guide us to nurture and guide them in Your ways, that they may grow in faith and love.

ON MY HEART TODAY:

GET CREATIVE:

What an honor it is to be a tiny somebody's everything.

LORD, THANK YOU:

MY PRAISE TO GOD:

I am calm and at peace

PRAYER REQUESTS:

ABOUT US

At Skrybe, our mission is to educate and inspire readers of all ages with meaningful and empowering content. We believe in the power of words to transform lives, and we strive to publish books that make a positive impact on the world.

We are committed to producing books of the highest quality, and we are dedicated to building lasting relationships with our authors, readers, and partners.

We also believe in giving back to our community. That's why we donate 5% of our net profits to charity, helping to make a difference in the lives of those who need it most.

Join our Skrybe community and subscribe to our mailing list to receive exclusive offers, inspiring content, and freebies that will help you on your personal growth and spiritual journey.

https://urlgeni.us/subscribetoskrybe

Follow the link or scan the QR code to join our mailing list

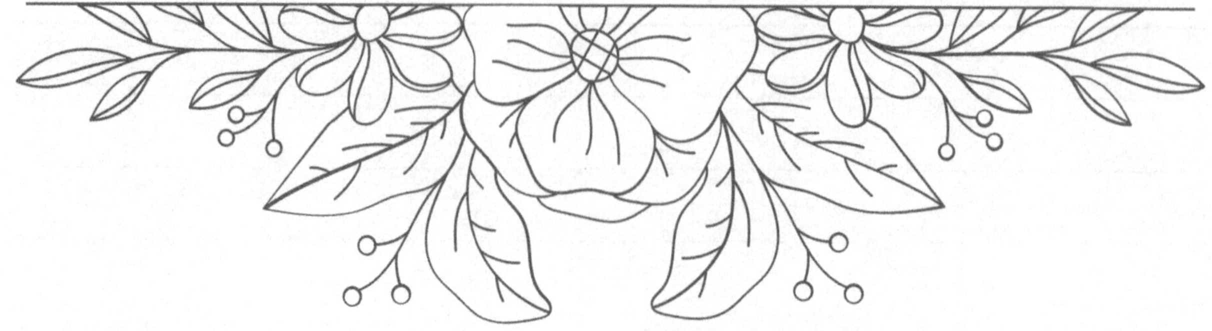

ALSO BY: SKRYBE

Are you looking for a way to deepen your spiritual journey with Christ and stay connected to your faith in your everyday life?

This beautifully designed journal is the perfect tool for women of God, who want to strengthen their identity in Christ and be empowered and affirmed in their faith.

- A beautiful and vibrant cover with hand-painted watercolor floral designs and the bible verse, "I am a Daughter of the King," from 2 Corinthians 6:18
- 8.5 x 5.5 inches, the ideal size to conveniently carry in your purse or backpack
- 128 blank wide-ruled pages, perfect for recording your daily prayers and reflecting on your spiritual growth
- Every other double page features a different bible verse to inspire and empower you. No repeated verses!
- Elegant floral interior design for beautiful bible journaling
- Designed to last, allowing you to look back on your path of spiritual growth for years to come

AVAILABLE ON AMAZON:

https://mybook.to/iamadaughteroftheking

ALSO BY: **SKRYBE**

Are you seeking a powerful tool to ignite your spiritual journey? Skrybe proudly presents a prayer journal for men — a rustic and masculine notebook crafted specifically for you. Embrace your identity as a Son of the King and embark on a transformative experience.

- A rustic and masculine cover design, exuding strength and authenticity, featuring the quote "I am a Son of the King" from 2 Corinthians 6:18
- Conveniently sized at 8.5 x 5.5 inches, making it easy to carry in your briefcase, backpack, or duffel bag
- 128 pages of lined paper, providing ample space to record prayers, and reflect on your spiritual journey
- Inspiring and empowering scripture verses on every other double page, guiding and uplifting you throughout your daily reflections
- Thoughtfully designed interior with a masculine touch, creating an inviting atmosphere for your Bible journaling and personal notes
- Crafted with durability in mind, ensuring that this prayer journal becomes a cherished companion for years to come, capturing your path of spiritual growth

AVAILABLE ON AMAZON:

https://mybook.to/iamasonoftheking

Made in the USA
Columbia, SC
17 December 2025